A Christmas Musical for Kids

Script & Lyrics by
Martha Bolton

Music by
Dennis Allen

Singer's Edition

PUBLISHING COMPANY

KANSAS CITY, MO 64141

Contents

Characters

*Solo or Ensemble Singer

*Snowflake	boy or girl
Director	man or woman
*Zeke	boy
Miss Eunice	girl or woman
Messenger	boy or girl
*Bully No. 1	boy (could be played by a girl)
*Bully No. 2	boy (could be played by a girl)
*Bully No. 3	boy (could be played by a girl)
Grandpa Shepherd	boy or man
Reuben	older boy or man
Angel	boy or girl
Bully's Mom	older girl or woman
*Sheep No. 1	boy or girl

Non-speaking Roles

Students

Mary

Joseph

What a Night!

with
O Come, Little Children
O Come, All Ye Faithful

MARTHA BOLTON

DENNIS ALLEN
Arranged by Dennis Allen

7

8

ho - ly Lamb, the great I Am, Was born this night in

Beth - le - hem!_____ O_____ what a night!

O_____ what a night! O

*"O Come, All Ye Faithful"

come, all ye faith - ful, joy - ful and tri -

um - phant. O come ye, O come_____ ye to

Beth - le - hem. Come and be -

hold Him— born the King of an - gels! O

come, let us a - dore Him! O come, let us a -

dore   Him!   O   come,   let   us   a -   dore   Him—

Christ,_____ the Lord!

what a night!_____   O_____ what a night!_____ What a night!

SCENE 1

(House lights go dark. Slowly stage lights up at right and follow spot on curtained partition. Snowflake pokes his or her head out through opening in curtain, looks at audience.

SNOWFLAKE: *(gasps)* Yikes! *(disappearing behind curtain)* Miss Sanders… *(or name of Director)* Did you see how many people are out there in the audience?

DIRECTOR: *(poking her head out from behind the curtain)* Yes. Isn't it great?

SNOWFLAKE: *(poking his head out again)* Great? Great? O…my agent's gonna hear about this!

DIRECTOR: Just think, Snowflake. All these people came tonight to hear <u>you</u> tell <u>your</u> story.

SNOWFLAKE: Tell 'em to wait 'til the movie comes out. *(disappearing behind the curtain)*

DIRECTOR: *(pulling him back through the curtain)* O come on, Snowflake. You've gotta go out there. You have an amazing story to tell and all these people gave up a night of holiday shopping just to hear you tell it. Now go!

SNOWFLAKE: *(stumbling onto stage)* But...but...*(nervously assessing the crowd)* Uh...hi...uh...my name is...uh...um... well...

DIRECTOR: *(from offstage)* Snowflake.

SNOWFLAKE: Uh...yeah...that's it. Snowflake. My name is Snowflake. I would've preferred the name "Rocky" *(or Rochelle),* but nobody asked me. Anyway, this is my story...my tale, so to speak.

It's...uh...about a night long ago when I, well...sort of wandered off from the flock. *(quickly)* But it wasn't my fault! Honest! See, there was this kid, Zekiahoboanezzer. We called him Zeke for short...we had to. It was either that or we'd all get tongue whiplash. Zeke was a nice kid and all, but this shepherd gig just wasn't his thing. See...*(Director pokes head through the curtain, give the "hurry up" sign and clears throat)* What? O...I think the director wants me to hurry up.

DIRECTOR: It's only supposed to be a forty-minute show...*(back behind curtain)*

SNOWFLAKE: All right. All right. I'm hurrying. Like I said before, my name's Snowflake and I belong to this flock of sheep. *(pointing to sheep choir who "wave" to audience)* And sheep have to be watched by shepherds. *(music begins)*
My shepherd was Zeke, the kid I was telling you about. That's him over there. *(pointing to Zeke)* He's a pretty nice guy, but he had a lot to learn about shepherding... and obedience. 'Course sheep have that down pat. We're very obedient animals...well, most of the time. *(Snowflake remains at stage right during song)*

Follow the Shepherd

MARTHA BOLTON

DENNIS ALLEN
Arranged by Dennis Allen

As before ♩ = ca. 84 ㉟

We fol - low our shep- herd, stay close by his

SHEEP #1: One more time!

50's rock ♩ = ca. 140 ㊸

We will fol-low him, we will fol-low where___ he

side. She- bop, she- bop, she- bop, she- bop!

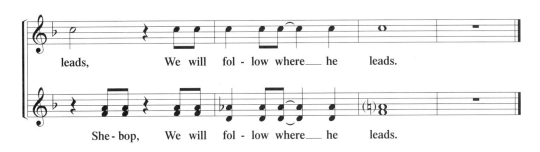

leads, We will fol - low where___ he leads.

She- bop, We will fol - low where___ he leads.

SNOWFLAKE: *(from stage right)* All right…so maybe I don't blame Zeke for not wanting to be a shepherd. Sheep can be a pain sometimes. And, there's the weather, too. A shepherd has to be out in the rain a lot. Sheep don't like that either. You know what water does to wool. And when you're a shepherd you always have to keep watch, making sure none of the sheep wander off. So, it's no wonder Zeke had other careers in mind. 'Course he didn't tell anybody how he felt…until one day…he couldn't hide it any longer.

(lights down at right, exit Snowflake)

SEGUE #1

SCENE 2

(Lights up on classroom setting at stage left. A few students, including Zeke and the three Bullies, are sitting in chairs and desks. Miss Eunice is standing in front of a chalkboard. On the board is written: CAREER DAY)

SFX: School bell

MISS EUNICE: Class…class. As you know, today we're going to be discussing career choices. Zeke, we'll start with you. Please stand and tell us what it is you want to be when you grow up.

(Zeke stands)

BULLY #1: We already know what he's going to be. He's gonna be a shepherd just like his old man. *(bullies laugh)* …and his father before him…and his father before him. That's all he <u>can</u> be. A shepherd. A lowly ol', no good shepherd.

ZEKE: I don't have to be a shepherd if I don't wanna be one. Why, I could be…I could be…a policeman.

BULLY #2: *(sarcastically)* O yeah, a shepherd boy would make a great cop! *(laughs)*

BULLY #3: He could catch all the criminals on the lam…get it? The lam?

(Bullies laugh and make baaing noises)

MISS EUNICE: Class…class…now, that's enough!

ZEKE: *(to the bullies)* Laugh all you want, but I am <u>not</u> going to be a shepherd.

BULLY #3: *(mockingly)* But then who'd watch wittle Snowflake?

BULLY #2: Yeah. Everybody knows it takes a <u>flake</u> to watch a <u>flake</u>!

MISS EUNICE: Now boys, we'll have none of that. Zeke's right. He can be whatever he wants to be when he grows up. *(music begins)*

ZEKE: Yeah. Snowflake'll get along just fine without me.

When I Grow Up

MARTHA BOLTON

DENNIS ALLEN
Arranged by Dennis Allen

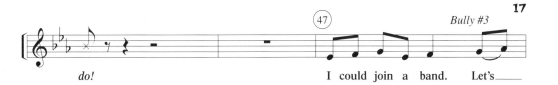

do!   I could join a band. Let's___

all give a hand for Zeke   and the flakes!___

(Bullies laugh and make baaing sounds)

MISS EUNICE: Class! Class! That's enough! If Zeke doesn't want to be a shepherd, he doesn't have to…

(enter messenger with note)

MESSENGER: Pardon me, Miss Eunice. I have a message here for someone named…Zeke. *(hands note to Miss Eunice)*

MISS EUNICE: A message? Let's see here. It's from your father, Zeke. He says to come straight home after school. You have to watch the sheep.

(students laugh and taunt)

BULLIES: *(in sing-songy style)* You have to watch the sheep…you have to watch the sheep…you have to watch the sheep…*(fading)*

(lights down at stage left)
(lights up at stage right as Snowflake enters)

SNOWFLAKE: *(to audience, from stage right)* Well, Zeke was the laughing stock of the whole class. But God had a special plan for Zeke's life. He had something very important for him to do on a very special night. A night that was about to change history.

(lights go down at right)

SEGUE #2

SCENE 3

(Lights up at center stage where Zeke, Reuben, Grandpa Shepherd, a few shepherds and some sheep are standing or sitting by a campfire.

NOTE: Night sound effects may be used in the background.
See PRODUCTION NOTES for resource.)

REUBEN: What are ya doin', Zeke?

ZEKE: Nothing, Dad. Just sittin' here thinking. *(pause)* The stars over Bethlehem are sure bright tonight, aren't they?

REUBEN: They've been growing brighter and brighter every night…like something special is about to happen.

ZEKE: What do you think it is?

REUBEN: I don't know. We'll just have to wait and see.

ZEKE: *(a beat)* Dad, can I ask you something?

REUBEN: Of course, Son.

ZEKE: Would it hurt your feelings if I told you I didn't want to be a shepherd?

REUBEN: You can be whatever you want to be, Zeke. But there's nothing wrong with being a shepherd, either.

ZEKE: I know. But it just isn't exciting enough for me.

REUBEN: Not exciting? Are you kidding? Come here, Zeke. I think it's time you learned just how exciting shepherding is. *(to other shepherds)* What'dya say, guys? Think it's time for Tales From the Flock?

(music begins)

Tales from the Flock

MARTHA BOLTON

DENNIS ALLEN
Arranged by Dennis Allen

REUBEN: Well, goodnight, Son. We'll see you in the morning.

SFX: howling of wolves, growling, owls hooting
(SEE PRODUCTION NOTES)

ZEKE: *(nervously)* You're going to sleep now?

REUBEN: Well, it's getting late. Besides, being a shepherd is boring, remember? Good luck on your watch tonight, Son.

ZEKE: Yeah....uh...good night.

(Reuben and all the other shepherds lie down to sleep; Zeke sits by campfire and continues to look around anxiously)

SFX: howling of wolves, growling, owls hooting

ZEKE: Dad?!

REUBEN: Yes, son?

ZEKE: Uh...would you mind keeping watch with me?

REUBEN: You're not....uh...bored, are you?

ZEKE: *(high pitched, nervously)* No. I just don't spend enough quality time with you, that's all.

REUBEN: All right. I'll watch with you.

SFX: night sounds

REUBEN: Grandpa...?

GRANDPA: Eh?

REUBEN: Would you mind keeping watch with Zeke and me?

GRANDPA: A watch? I don't need no watch. Already got three of 'em now that don't work.

ZEKE: *(to Reuben)* It's all right, Dad. I'll keep watch. You and Grandpa go on to sleep.

REUBEN: You sure?

ZEKE: Yeah. I'll be fine.

REUBEN: Well, if you need anything, we'll be right here. But whatever you do, don't fall asleep. The sheep are depending on you.

ZEKE: I know, Dad. *(yawning)* I know.
(music begins)

O Little Town of Bethlehem

PHILLIPS BROOKS

LEWIS H. REDNER
Arranged by Dennis Allen

O

lit - tle town of Beth - le - hem, How still we____ see thee

lie! A - bove thy deep and dream - less sleep The

si - lent____ stars go by. Yet in thy dark streets

shin - eth The ev - er - last - ing Light; The

hopes and fears of all the years Are met in thee to -

night.

For Christ is born of Mar - y; And, gath - ered— all a - bove, While mor - tals sleep, the an - gels keep Their watch of— won - d'ring love. O morn - ing stars, to - geth - er Pro - claim the ho - ly birth; And prais - es sing to God, the King, And peace to men on earth.

(shepherds are snoring loudly)

ZEKE: *(beginning to get drowsy)* Yeah…the stars sure are bright tonight…I'm glad. They'll help keep me awake. Yeah…I'm gonna stay awake…wide…*(begins snoring)*

SNOWFLAKE: *(crossing to center stage)* Listen to all that growling. And they're worried about bears? Well, as you can see, no one was watching me. So, being the curious lamb that I am, I started wandering farther…and father…and farther…*(Zeke snores louder)*…I said, hey, I'm wandering now…No, really. I'm going…*(Zeke snorts really loud!)* O well, I figured I'd be back by morning before Zeke ever knew I was gone.

(lights down at center, exit Snowflake)

SEGUE #3

Scene 4

(Lights up at center. Zeke and the other shepherds are fast asleep by the campfire.)

ZEKE: *(waking up suddenly)* O no! It's morning! I must've fallen asleep. I was supposed to watch the sheep and I fell asleep. Let's see....*(begins to count the sheep...)* *(after a few beats)* 96...97...98...99...O no, one's missing! It's Snowflake! Snowflake's gone!

(Reuben and other shepherds wake up...)

REUBEN: What's the matter, Son?

ZEKE: Snowflake's gone. I counted all the sheep and Snowflake's missing!

GRANDPA: How could he be missing? You were watching him last night, weren't you?

ZEKE: I fell asleep...but only for a little while. An hour tops. Maybe two. No more than four...I'm sure of that. O Dad. I'm really sorry!

REUBEN: We'll spread out and help you look for him.

(shepherds start calling for Snowflake....then exit)

ZEKE: Snowflake! Snowflake! *(cupping his hand over his mouth; pacing, calling)* Snooooooowwwwwwflaaaaaaaaaake!!

(enter Bullies from left)

BULLY #1: *(mockingly)* Hey, you! Shepherd boy!

ZEKE: *(looking around)* Who me?

BULLY #2: Yeah...you. Zeke, the Geek.

ZEKE: I'm not looking for any trouble, guys. I'm just trying to find Snowflake.

BULLY #3: If you're looking for a flake, why don't you just look in a mirror?

(Bullies laugh!! Music begins)

Our Turf

MARTHA BOLTON

DENNIS ALLEN
Arranged by Dennis Allen

This is our____ turf! So lis-ten up good! Your sheep got-ta go,____ can't graze in our 'hood! This is our____ turf! No need to get rough,__ I'm just pass-in' through, I'll be on my way.__ *So light-en up, dudes!*____

ZEKE: *(calls out)* Snowflake!...Snowflake!...Where are you...*(etc.)*

This is our____ turf! It's o-ver your head. We told you to *scram!*__ Now do what we said! This is our____ turf! You're not wel-come here,____ so,

don't be a fool!_____ We'd look for your lamb..._____

but we're al - ler - gic to wool!_____

BULLY #3: Wait!
(cupping his ear with his hand)
I think I hear wittle Snowflaky-waky now!

BULLY #2: (getting
down on all fours)
Baaaa! Baaaa!

(more laughing,
poking fun)

I know I'm not cool._____ I know I'm not tough,_____ But

Snow-flake's my lamb,_____ and e - nough is e - nough!_____

BULLY #1: Says who?

ZEKE: (standing firm) Says me! You don't scare me. I'm gonna search every inch of this place 'til I find him and that's final!!

BULLIES' MOM: (from offstage) Bufus....Dufus.....Rufus. You boys get home right now and do your chores. And you better not be up to any mischief.

ZEKE: Hey, guys. I think your mommy's calling you!

BULLY #2: Yeah...well....we'll be back for you!

ZEKE: (sarcastically) Ooooo, I'm shaking in my sandals.

BULLIES: Come on, guys. Yeah, let's go. (ad lib.)

Bullies exit left

ZEKE: *(hyperventilating)* Whew! That was close. Thought I was gonna be road pizza. O....I'd better hurry. Anything could happen to a lamb all alone out here. *(as he exits)* Snowflake! Snowflake!!! *(fading, exits)*

(lights up stage right)

SNOWFLAKE: *(at stage right, to the audience)* You know, none of this would've happened if he had just obeyed his father and watched me in the first place. But Zeke still had a lot to learn. So, the shepherds looked for me all morning, all afternoon, and when nighttime came, they still hadn't found me. When I get lost, I really get lost. But that night wasn't going to be any ordinary night...as Zeke was about to find out.

(lights down stage right)

ZEKE: *(entering from left, crossing to center)* Snowflake!! Snowflake!!!

(suddenly a bright light shines on Zeke)

SFX: angel's appearance

ZEKE: Snowflake?

(angel enters from up stage)

ZEKE: Whoa! You're not Snowflake. You're an angel! The others are never gonna believe this!

ANGEL: Fear not! For behold I bring you good tidings of great joy, which shall be to all people. For unto you is born this day in the city of David, a Savior which is Christ the Lord. And this shall be a sign unto you. Ye shall find the babe wrapped in swaddling clothes, lying in a manger.

(angel exits up stage)

ZEKE: A Savior? Born in Bethlehem? I've gotta go tell the others!

(bright light down; exit Zeke left)
(lights down center)

SEGUE #4

Scene 5

(Lights up at stage left...the Bullies front porch. They're all sweeping and wearing frilly aprons. Enter Zeke from left. His face "glows" SEE PRODUCTION NOTES. Zeke is running....stopping for a second, exhausted)

BULLY #1: Hey, isn't he that shepherd boy?

BULLY #2: Yeah. I thought we told him to beat it.

BULLY #1: Let's show him who's in charge around here.

BULLY #3: Wait a minute. We can't let him see us doing...housework and wearing these aprons.

BULLY #1: O yeah.

BULLY #2: Here...hide the brooms....and let's take off these stupid aprons.

BULLY #1: I can't get mine untied.

BULLY #2: Me neither.

BULLY #3: Hey, wait a minute. Are you sure that's the same guy? He looks....different.

BULLY #1: Yeah. What's with that glow on his face?

BULLY #2: I don't know. Maybe he's like radioactive or something.

BULLY #3: I think we'd better leave him alone.

BULLY #1: I think you guys have been reading too many science fiction scrolls. He probably just went to one of those, you know, tanning salons.
(to Zeke) Hey....you...shepherd boy! Did you find your wittle sheepy weepy?

ZEKE: *(pacing frantically)* I can't talk now, guys. I'm on my way to see a king!

BULLY #3: A king? *(laughs)* You?

BULLY #2: Now, why would a king want to see you?

ZEKE: I don't know, but an angel came and told me <u>all</u> about him.

BULLY #1: An angel? You…saw an angel?

BULLY #2: Well, he is glowing.

BULLY #3: *(backing off)* And I still don't think we should mess with someone who glows.

(enter Bullies' Mom from left)

BULLIES' MOM: You boys quit your socializing and get back to work! We've got a lot to do…*(starting to exit, then noticing Zeke)* Say, kid, do you know you're glowing? I'd have that checked out if I were you.

BULLY #1: Mom, he says he's seen an angel.

BULLIES' MOM: There's an angel out here? You boys would say anything to get out of work! Here. Now…get busy!

(exit Mom left)

ZEKE: *(to Bullies)* You know, it's funny. All these years I though <u>you</u> were the cool ones, but someone who sees an angel and gets invited to a King's birthday? Now that's cool. *(music begins)* By the way, nice aprons.

You're Cool

MARTHA BOLTON

DENNIS ALLEN
Arranged by Dennis Allen

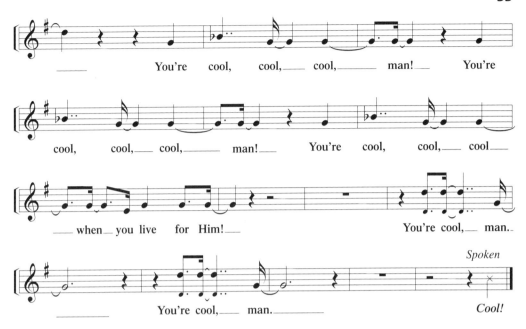

You're cool, cool, cool, man! You're cool, cool, cool, man! You're cool, cool, cool when you live for Him! You're cool, man. You're cool, man. *Cool!*

(lights down at left)

SEGUE #5

Scene 6

(Lights up at center. Reuben and the other shepherds are gathering their belongings. Enter Zeke excitedly.)

ZEKE: Dad! Dad! Did you see him? Did you see the angel?

REUBEN: I sure did! We all did. We're going to Bethlehem now. You coming with us?

ZEKE: You better believe it! But, wait a minute, Dad. What about Snowflake?

REUBEN: I'm sorry, Son. But if Snowflake hasn't turned up by now, *(music begins)* I'm afraid…

ZEKE: You mean?…

REUBEN: *(trying to console Zeke)* Come on… let's go to Bethlehem. All we can do is hope and pray Snowflake will be all right.

(lights down at center)

Away in a Manger
with
Silent Night!

Anonymous and
JOHN THOMAS McFARLAND

JAMES R. MURRAY
Arranged by Dennis Allen

Tenderly ♩ = ca. 94

Choir *mf*

A -

way in a man-ger, no crib for a bed, The

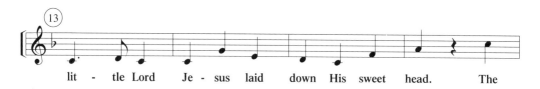

lit - tle Lord Je - sus laid down His sweet head. The

stars in the sky___ looked down where He lay, The

lit - tle Lord Je - sus a - sleep on the hay.

Be

near me, Lord Je - sus; I ask Thee to stay Close

by me for - ev - er, and love me, I pray. Bless

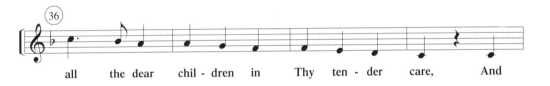

all the dear chil - dren in Thy ten - der care, And

fit us for heav - en, to live with Thee there, And

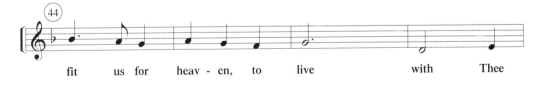

fit us for heav - en, to live with Thee

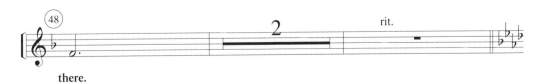

there.

*"Silent Night!"

Si - lent night! ho - ly night!

All is calm, all is bright

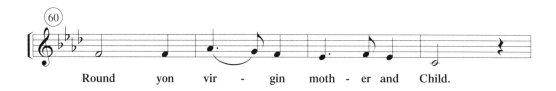

Round yon vir - gin moth - er and Child.

Ho - ly In - fant, so ten - der and mild,

Sleep in heav - en - ly peace;_____

Sleep_____ in heav - en - ly peace.

Scene 7

(Lights up at right where there is a manger scene; Mary, Joseph, Baby Jesus, Zeke and the other shepherds enter and gather around the manger)

REUBEN: He's beautiful, isn't He, Son?

ZEKE: Yeah. Imagine a King sleeping in a manger.

REUBEN: He's God's own Lamb...

(enter Bullies and Snowflake)

and speaking of lambs...

ZEKE: What?

BULLY #1: *(to Zeke)* Hey...uh....Zeke. I think we found something that belongs to you.

ZEKE: *(hugging Snowflake)* Snowflake?! *(to Bullies)* How'd you find him? *(to Snowflake)* Boy, am I glad to see you. *(to Bullies)* Hey, thanks guys. How come...well.... I mean this is so unlike you. What made you change?

BULLY #2: I don't know. Maybe it was the fact that you're...you know...glowing.

BULLY #3: That, and something just told us this was a good night for peace and goodwill toward men.

ZEKE: But how in the world did you find us here...in a stable?

BULLY #2: *(pointing skyward)* Let's just say someone left a light on for us. *(Bullies ad lib. about the star)*

(music begins)

SNOWFLAKE: *(to Zeke)* Sorry I wandered off.

ZEKE: That's okay, Snowflake. The important thing is that you're home where you belong.

(lights down at right)

Where I Belong

MARTHA BOLTON

DENNIS ALLEN
Arranged by Dennis Allen

on - ly one me,_____ u - nique as can be._____
one of a kind_____ and I've been as - signed_____ To

No one else can do what I can._____ When-
be_____ all He wants me to be._____ I

ev - er He calls,_____ I'll give Him my all._____ I'm
won't go a - stray,_____ for - ev - er I'll stay._____ For

part of His won - der - ful plan._____
He is de - pend - ing on me._____ When I'm

where I be - long,_____ God can use__ me; When I'm

SCENE 8

(Lights up at right. Scene opens as Snowflake walks through curtain at right and addresses the audience)

SNOWFLAKE: So there you have it, folks. That's my tale and it's the truth. Every last bit of it. And I should know, 'cause I was there. I saw the manger, and Baby Jesus, the Savior of the world, lying right there in it! What a night!

DIRECTOR: *(poking her head through curtain)* See, that wasn't so bad, was it?

SNOWFLAKE: No. Actually, it was kinda fun. I love stories with a happy ending.

ZEKE: *(from offstage)* Hey, where's Snowflake?

REUBEN: *(from offstage)* Don't tell me you lost him again.

ZEKE: *(from offstage)* He was here a minute ago... Snowflake! Snowflake!!

SNOWFLAKE: Over here, guys.

ZEKE: *(enter from left, crossing to Snowflake)* Snowflake! What are you doing?

SNOWFLAKE: Sorry. I was just talking to the people here, telling 'em about you and the angel and Baby Jesus and...

ZEKE: Look, if I'm going to be your shepherd, you've gotta quit wandering off like this. It's dangerous out there and....

SNOWFLAKE: What was that you said?

ZEKE: I said it's dangerous out there and...

SNOWFLAKE: No, that other part...about being my shepherd. Does that mean...?

ZEKE: Well, I've been doing a lot of thinking...

SNOWFLAKE: *(anxiously)* And?

ZEKE: And I guess I've sort of decided that....

SNOWFLAKE: Yes...? Yes...?

ZEKE: Well, that being a shepherd isn't so bad after all. In fact, it's pretty cool. Ya know, if I hadn't been a shepherd, I wouldn't have seen an angel...and I might not have ever gotten to see God's greatest Gift...ever!

SNOWFLAKE: Yeah! God's got something special for all those who are in the right place at the right time. Huh, Zeke?

ZEKE: Right, Snowflake. Let's both try to remember that!!

(all stage lights up, enter entire cast and choir)
(music begins)

Finale

including
Where I Belong
What a Night!
Go, Tell It on the Mountain

Arranged by Dennis Allen

44

O_____ what a night!

*"Go, Tell It on the Mountain"

Go, tell it on the moun - tain, O - ver the hills and

ev - ery - where; Go, tell it on the moun - tain That

Je - sus Christ___ is born! Go, tell it on the

moun - tain, O - ver the hills and ev - ery - where;

Go, tell it on the moun - tain That Je - sus

Christ_____ is born! Christ is born!

Opt. divisi

Christ is born! Christ is born!